PUBLISHED by PARABLES
Earthly Stories with a Heavenly Meaning

Life As I Know It

By
Bernie Hambrice

Earthly Stories with a Heavenly Meaning

Bernie Hambrice
Life As I Know It

Published By Parables
December, 2020

All Rights Reserved. No part of this book may be reproduced or utilized in any form or by any means, electronic or mechanical, including photocopying, recording, or by any information storage and retrieval system, without permission in writing from the author.

    ISBN 978-0-9974392-9-8
    Printed in the United States of America

Readers should be aware that Internet Web sites offered as citations and/or sources for further information may have been changed or disappeared between the time this was written and the time it is read.

LIFE AS I KNOW IT

By
Bernie Hambrice

PUBLISHED by PARABLES
Earthly Stories with a Heavenly Meaning

Bernie Hambrice

LIFE

I was born on November 1, 1937 in Haynesville, Louisiana. Of course, I don't remember a whole lot about it, but based on the facts as told to me, the story goes as follows. My Mom, Fern Carroll McDaniel, went into labor with me on October 31, Halloween, so she thought that she would have a black cat, but instead got a red headed witch.

Life was rough for my parents at that time. It was the great depression. Dad, Meak B. McDaniel, had a broken leg. After my birth, my parents stayed with my aunt and uncle in Homer, Louisiana. Mom had pictures of me lying in a wicker clothes basket. That was my bed. We also stayed for a short time with my paternal grandparents, Lee and Willie Belle McDaniel, in Arkansas prior to that.

When I was about one year old, my Dad was in a logging accident. He was on top of a load of logs stacked on the bed of a truck when the chain holding them in place snapped. He fell and the load of logs fell on his legs, breaking both of them. He was in a body cast from just under his arms to the tips of his toes. Of course, back in that time, there was no such thing as air conditioning. You can imagine how hot, sweaty, and uncomfortable that had to be. One of my favorite stories about that is when my Mom put me up in the bed with him. I was eating crackers; the crumbs got in the bed and you can imagine what happened. The crumbs got down inside of the body cast. I can only imagine that even though I was their only child, I definitely wasn't his favorite.

We were so poor at that time. My Mom told me that things were very bleak. I think that is actually when we moved in my aunt and uncle and their two children, Nanella and John (Sonny). Just before Christmas that year things were pretty dismal. My parents worried that I would not have a Christmas. My Mom got a job with very little pay working in

Life As I Know It

a store, but was able to buy me a little red rocker for Santa to bring. She was really a teacher, but could not go out and work full time with my Dad in the body cast. I feel very special to have such loving and caring parents.

When I was two years old, Dad had a job with Chambers Oil Company driving a truck. He was sent to south Louisiana with a load of oil, but was suppose to remain in Chalmette for a two month period. My Mom, much as she didn't want to, decided to accompany him. We came to Chalmette in July 1940 and here we stayed.

My first memories of life in Chalmette, was living in half of a double shotgun house on the street close to Meraux School (now the School Board office). Back then, it wasn't really a street. Living next door to us was a girl destined to be my best friend. Her name was Florence Corne, but her family called her Ta Tee. She was 16 days younger than I. We were constantly together. She had been a late in life baby for her parents. Her mother was in poor health, so she stayed with us a lot. I was still an only child and her parents had several (I think all of them were boys) and she was the youngest.

We moved into another half house on the corner of St. Bernard Highway and what later became Buffon Street. The Palamas who owned the house, lived in the other half. This was during World War II. I can remember that my bed was an army cot in the same room with my parents. Some times at night, an air raid siren would sound which meant that no lights were to be on. I would be on my cot with a flashlight on under the covers so that I would not be afraid. To a young child this was pretty scary.

During that period of time, the Palamas sold sandwiches for lunches to the students at Meraux School. Their daughter, Marie, would go over to the school each morning and into the classrooms to take orders. The sandwiches were what we call Po Boys. They were ten cents each. They smelled wonderful and I could hardly wait until I was old enough to go to school and I could have one of those wonderful sandwiches each day.

I spent a lot of time at the school even before I was old enough to go. My Mom taught me to roller skate at the school. Inside, there was a large auditorium with terrazzo floors and it was slanted like a modern day movie theater. During the summer, there were no seats in there, I would stand up against the back wall where the floor was elevated and push off towards the front. That is how I first learned to roller skate. At that time St. Bernard had dirt roads and no sidewalks so I felt blessed to have access to the school. Thanks goodness for the Palamas and their jobs which gave me access to the school. We moved from there to a larger place before I started school.

We moved into an apartment in what would later become the Fradella House, but Ta Tee and I still stayed together most of the time. We could walk from our house to theirs even though we had to cross Paris Road. Back then there was not many people or cars in St. Bernard Parish. Friends of my parents had a car with a rumble seat in the back. My parents did not own a car at that time and it was so exciting to ride in the rumble seat. It was like riding in a convertible with the top down. I can remember Ta Tee and me standing in the open field behind Meraux School and watching the big kids at recess. We were all of five at that time.

Finally the big day came when we started school. There was only one class at each grade level and so the two of us were in the same class. Our first grade (there was no kindergarten back in the old days) teacher was Mrs. Andre'. We thought that she was wonderful and she also had a son in our class. Mrs. Andre' died during that school year and this was my first experience with death. We all felt so sorry for our friend Jimmy. We had a temporary teacher take her place in the classroom who refused the job full time because of one of the students. The teacher was Fern Carroll McDaniel, my mother. She refused the job because any time that she called on me to do or answer anything, I would whine, "I don't want to." She just couldn't take it. She actually thought that it was not good for me. I had a "boy friend" in the class, Roland Cutrer and we would sit and hold hands in class. That upset my Mom. I don't remember who the teacher was that took her place.

During second grade, I had a wonderful little old maid teacher, Miss Colomb. She let us get by with so much. I can remember one time when I wanted to go get a drink of water (which we were not suppose to leave class for) and I told her that I needed water because my tooth was loose (fib). I was standing at the water fountain getting water when

Life As I Know It

the fire breathing dragon principal, Miss Duplantis, came up. She wanted to know why I was out of class. I told her the same story. She wanted to know which tooth. I pointed out one that was just beginning to be loose. She reached in my mouth with her steam roller hands and yanked and pulled until she got that tooth out. It hurt so much that I never tried that again.

It was when I was seven that my brother, Patrick Lee McDaniel, was born. It was wonderful to have an actual sibling. He was the joy of my life. I still had my best friend, but now I also had a brother. We played with him constantly and I think that I thought that he was my own private property.

I can remember when we heard on the radio, there were no televisions back then, that the war had ended. My mom and Ta Tee's mom let us stay home from school. We stood in the field and watched all of the other kids that had to go to school that day. The next day was declared a holiday, so we were able to really enjoy the end of World War II. That was all the war meant to me. My only memories of it were the black outs and the rationing stamps that we had to use to purchase sugar and other commodities. We also had savings books. You had to fill it with stamps and once it was filled, you would trade it in for a war bond. These stamps were ten cents each and it took a long time to fill the book. I can remember walking to the tiny post office on St. Bernard Highway and buying one stamp at a time. The post office was managed by two old maid sisters, the Misses Colomb, whose sister was my teacher.

When we were nine years old, my friend Ta Tee discovered a lump in the upper part of her right arm. That was the first time that I heard the dreaded word cancer. All I really knew was that she had a lump that grew quite large. She finally had to go to the hospital for surgery. They were going to try to cut the lump out, but they told her that there was a possibility that they might have to amputate her arm. I remember her mom telling my mom how Ta Tee cried in her hospital bed when they told her that. As she lay there crying, she told them in a broken voice, that if they didn't have to cut her arm off that she would go to church every day. She was trying to bargain with God. Her dad fell across her and the bed and crying softly that he would go with her. There were no bargains to be made. They had to amputate her arm to try to save her life. After she returned home. She was still my best friend, but she became a different person. I didn't realize that her body was slowly being eaten away with cancer. She died when we were ten years old. This was my second experience with death. It was very hard seeing my best friend being laid out in a casket and knowing that never again could we share secrets, pranks, or even chicken pox, which we had at the same time.

Life for me went on, but on a different scale. I missed my best friend so much. It was during this time that the Beard family moved in an apartment in the same house with us. The parents, Mary and Bob, had 2 children, Mary and Bobby. We were friends, but they could never replace Ta Tee.

When I was in the seventh grade (in those days Meraux School went from first to seventh grade) my teacher was the principal Miss Duplantis. I was sitting in class one day when I saw Geniveve Coig and Mary Beard in the hallway motioning to Miss Duplantis. I thought how funny it was to see Mary Beard at school with her hair up in rollers because women just didn't go our in public looking like that. They went into the principal's office. After a short time, Miss Duplantis came out and told me that I was needed at home and that the two ladies were going to take me there. I thought that was odd because I walked to and from school by myself every day. This was when I got my third taste of death and the bitterest one yet. I was told that my brother Pat had been killed. He was only five years old.

He had been out riding his bike and had gone to the Roberts' house down the street to play with Clora, their daughter, who was the same age. Mom went out to call him for lunch. He didn't answer her. She saw his bike in a shallow ditch on the side of their home. She thought that he was trying to hide from her because he didn't want to go home. When she got closer, she saw that his bike was bent out of shape. When the Roberts heard her yelling Pat's name, they came out of the house. Mr. Roberts picked Pat up in his arms. Pat took one last deep breath and then Harvey Roberts said that Pat was dead. I can imagine the disbelief and anguish that she must have felt because I too have felt that same loss with one of my own children. I thought that life would never be the same without Pat. He had been my baby and now he was gone. I cried myself to sleep for many nights. Here I was twelve years old and I had experienced the loss of three very important people in my life.

I finished 7th grade at Meraux School and from there I was to go to Arabi School for 8th grade. It was during that summer that my parents made their final move in Chalmette. They bought their house at #2 Keane Drive. They wanted a permanent place because Mother was expecting another baby. We were happy with our new house, but once again, I was an only child, It was a very lonely period in my life. Mom had my sister, Kathy, in August. I made friends in the neighborhood, but still felt the loss of Ta Tee and Pat so very much.

It was during my first year at Arabi that I met a tall, lanky boy named George Hambrice. He was in some of my classes at school and he and his family began attending our church. He seemed to be everywhere I was. I can remember how he use to bother me, so I would swing my purse (with a soft ball inside of it) at him. I actually tried my best to hurt him. He was already six feet tall. He told the other boys that if they sat by me on the bus he would beat them up. He pointed me out at church and told his mother that I was the girl that he was going to marry. Even though he was a terrible aggravation, he would come over to our house to play volleyball. I would pray to God to help me find the right man to marry when I got older, but please don't let it be George Hambrice. Now it was me trying to bargain with God. You would think that I might have learned that it wouldn't work.

Once I was 15, my parents would let me go out on group dating, at least 3 couples, to the drive-in theater. We would aways go with Walter and Billy Cure and their dates because they had a car that 6 of us could fit in. Before these group dates, George would walk from his house to my house (about a mile) and my mom would take us to the Arabi Show. We would have to find out what time the feature ended and she would come back to pick us up. We began to sit in church together and hold hands. At sixteen we were finally able to go out on actual dates, but then our lives changed drastically again.

One evening, George was over at our house playing Monopoly with my half sister, Elizabeth, and me. Then he announced at just sixteen years of age that he had joined the Army. His mom had gotten him a new birth certificate that showed him a year older than he really was.

Bernie Hambrice

He went into the Army during the Korean War and it was there in Korea that he celebrated his 17th birthday. While there, he contacted a disease called Hemophelmic Fever. We heard from his commanding officer that George had been airlifted and was in very grave danger. It was a hard time for all of us. He managed to survive and seemed to have no lasting effects.

During his next leave, he gave me a diamond engagement ring. I thought that I was so grown up. Here I was 17 years old and engaged. Needless to say that didn't last too long. I guess that is the reason that my parents agreed to it in the first place. We fought all the time. My parents hadn't given in easily about me accepting the ring. My Mom kept telling me that my junior and senior years in high school should be the happiest years of my school career. She said that if I was engaged and George was off somewhere in the Army, I would not be able to attend a lot of the events. I thought that I had all of the answers and who needed proms and all that stuff.

After we broke the engagement I did go to proms, but the one for my senior year, I went with George. By that time we were dating again, but not exclusively with each other. One night I was at the skating rink in Arabi and George came there. He told me that he had a set of rings and that did I know anyone who would want them. I told him that I didn't want them because they were yellow gold and I liked white gold. He didn't say anything, but the next week he came back with a new set of rings and this time they were white gold. We became engaged once again. I was not quite 19 years old.

On my 18th birthday Mom gave birth to my baby brother, Meak B. McDaniel, Jr. (Buddy). We had completed our family. Mom was nervous when she was pregnant with Buddy because she would be 40 years old when he was born. Everything turned out great. She said that he was my birthday present. I know that I got another birthday gift, but for the life of me I can't remember what it was.

On March 16, 1957, George and I were married at Chalmette Baptist Church. The reception was held at the home of my aunt and uncle, Katherine and Ralph Hanle. It was a wonderful wedding with one small exception. Buddy had mumps and chicken pox together for the wedding. It put quite a strain on my mother's nerves to have out of town company staying at our house, a really sick child, and her daughter getting married. She managed to survive with a tired smile on her face.

George was working at the Ingram Oil Refinery when we got married. There was a turn around going on at the refinery and they didn't want to let George have time off for the wedding. They finally agreed to giving the weekend off, but he had to work on Friday, the day of the wedding. We were able to go to Biloxi for the weekend, but had to get back on Sunday night so that he could go to work on Monday morning. I was working at Swift and Company District Office and had taken the next week off. I spent the time trying to put our apartment in order. I guess I had too much time to relax and bother George because 9 months and 19 days after our weddimg, I gave birth to our first child. Mark Edward Hambrice was born on January 4, 1958. We were thrilled and thought that he was the only baby on the face of the earth. When my Aunt Katherine called to ask about the baby, Kathy got on the phone and told her that I had a little boy. When asked what his name was, she replied, "Write or Scribble or something like that." Katherine was able to figure out that his name must be Mark.

About 2 months prior to Mark's birth, I was in the kitchen of our house on Fenelon Street baking cupcakes. There was suddenly a loud banging on the back door. I went to the door and there was my mother-in-law crying and screaming that Ingram Oil had just blown up and everyone there had been killed. George was at work at that time. I told her that she must be mistaken or that I would have heard something. I did what every young woman would do at a time like that. I called my mother and told her what had been said. Her response was that it probably wasn't true or it would have been on the news and for me to not get excited because I could go into labor and I hadn't been married 9 months yet. She later denied having ever told me that. There had been a fire, but only one person had been killed. I didn't hear from George until about 12 hours later, but I was able to calm down and not go into labor much to my mother's relief.

I always thought that Mark was a very special child. The month after he was born, we actually had snow to cover the ground in Chalmette – the first that I was able to remember seeing. Mom gave me directions and I was able to catch enough snow in a bowl to make my first ever snow ice cream. I was so proud of my son and took him everywhere so people could see this wonderful child of mine.

Again, I seemed to have too much time to relax and became pregnant again, but miscarried when I was about 3 months. We cried because to us it was a tragedy. But in a few months, I got pregnant again. We were living in a house on Livingston Drive between Keane and Gibbs. We had movies when I felt like I was so fat for Mark's second birthday party. I was about 3 months pregnant and still wearing straight skirts and weighed about 123 pounds. We were so excited about the coming child and marked off the days on the calendar to the due date.

During that summer, Mom, Dad, Kathy, and Buddy moved to Abilene, Texas and we moved into my parents home. It was while we were there that Fern Carroll Hambrice was born. She was due on July 27, and since Mark was born only 2 days after his due date, I thought surely that Fern woud be born before the end of July. Well, was I surprised! After 2 false alarms, toxema, and outgrowing all of my clothes and shoes, Fern was born on August 11, 1960. It was a breech birth and a really rough time. She definitely was worth all of the problems that I had experienced. She was a beautiful red headed baby and was named after my mother whose first name was Fern and her maiden name was Carroll. We felt that all was well with the world. We had a 2 ½ year old son and a new baby girl.

Mom and Dad loved Abilene, but they felt like Chalmette was home and their family was here. After living in Abilene for about a year, they moved back to their house in Chalmette and we moved to a house on Cochran Drive. Guess what! By the time that we moved away from there, I was pregnant again. It was when I was about six months pregnant that we bought our first house. It was 2416 Riverbend Drive. We thought that it was wonderful even though it was about 7 or 8 miles below Paris Road, which most people thought that it was so out of the way. But the first house that you purchase is wonderful no matter where it is.

Jerry Lee Hambrice was born on September 14, 1962, about 3 months after we moved in our house. He had white hair and was a very big baby. I thought that all was well because he was healthy. When he was almost 2 weeks old, I had to be rushed back to the hospital because of hemoraging. I had to have a D & C and was in the hospital for nearly a week. Now we had 3 beautiful children and were very satisfied. Life was very busy with 3 children, but I guess not busy enough because as you can guess, I got pregnant again. I just knew that this time I would have a girl. That would have given us 2 of each. But on March 5, 1965, Paul Daniel Hambrice was born. He was another red head. We loved him so much even though he wasn't the girl we were expecting. If ever there was a child that lived up to the reputation of Dennis the Menace, that was Paul. Now we had 4 children with the oldest being 8 years old.

You would think that by then we would have learned what was causing this population explosion, but we obviously hadn't figured it out or else we just enjoyed doing what comes naturally; but we soon found out that I was pregnant again. I was thrilled. I had been an only child so much of my life that I wanted a house full of children. But we faced reality and started figuring out the cost of a big family was astronomical, so George went to see a doctor during my pregnancy. That was a wild experience. After his surgery, George developed a major infection. He became so inflamed in his tender parts, that he was running a very high fever and could not even walk. We tried to call his doctor, but he was out of town. I finally had to call my OB to get him some help. George always blamed me for his problem.

On November 4, 1966, I gave birth to a beautiful girl that we named Holly Kay Hambrice. We knew then that our family was complete. My mother sighed with relief as she realized that this would be our last child. Holly also had very bright red hair. I laughed and said that she was our stoplight. Of course, I had 2 other stoplights, but I guess we just ran right on through them.

We knew that we had our family and were very satisfied with it. You can just imagine what fun we had with 5 children and the oldest one 9 years old. I can remember that one time I went shopping and of course, I had to take all 5 children. It was very hard to get a baby sitter crazy enough to stay with that many kids. I was in the elevator in Maison Blanche in the Gentilly Shopping Center. A man got on the elevator, looked around in disbelief and asked if they were all mine or did I run a nursery. He got off of the elevator at the next floor shaking his head. I just smiled, grabbed an elusive child, and went on with my shopping. I am not going to tell you that it was all fun and games. It was a terribly exhausting experience.

Seven months after Holly's birth our world, as we knew it, came to an end. One night I had gone to an activity for the Murphy Oil Corporation's social club (formerly Ingram Oil). My friend's brother and his girlfriend came over to babysit. They didn't know us very well. I was concerned about leaving the children with them, but they assured me that they could handle it.

While at the function, I saw a policeman come in and talk to people near the front door. It was just like the scene at Meraux School when they came to get me after my little brother had been killed. I saw them look over in my direction. Then someone came over and got me. They told me that my family needed me. I left in the squad car with the deputy. He told me that there had been a fire and one of my children was in the hospital. He didn't tell me anything else. When we got to the local hospital I ran in looking for my children. I didn't know which one I was looking for, but I knew that I had to find someone to send me in the right direction. As I passed people in the hall, I heard them whisper, "That is the mother." I was terrified, not knowing what I was going to find. A nurse came and took me by the arm. She led into a room and told me to wait for the doctor. I kept asking where my child was. Finally, a doctor came into the room. He looked sadly at me, shook his head and said "I'm sorry." Sorry for what? I couldn't understannd why they would not let me see my child. Then he told me as kindly as he could that my little boy Paul had died from smoke inhalation.

If I had thought that losing my little brother was the hardest thing that I had ever faced; I didn't have an inkling to what real pain was. To lose a child; a part of you, is the worse pain that I can ever imagine. That child had been a part of you; but now that part is dead – gone forever. I was told that they had gotten the other children out safely, but had forgotten Paul who was sleeping in the back bedroom. I remember screaming and telling them that I had reminded the baby sitters that I had 5 children. 1-2-3-4-5! How could they forget him? They only had to count to five. I was devestated. I wanted my other children. The deputy took me down to our house. At first we couldn't get anywhere near the house because of the fire trucks and cars where people had come to see what had happened. We were told that the children were with my parents at their house. Again I got into the squad car and was driven to Keane Drive. George and I had missed each other in the passing. I got to my Mom's house and when I saw my parents and my other children, I broke down completely. I was ready to die, but God had other plans for me.

The next few days were the hardest of my life. We went through the motions of living. Mom and George went to the funeral home to make arrangements. It was more than I could handle. The day of the wake, I tried every possible excuse to keep from going and seeing my child laid out in a casket. I thought about jumping off the furniture to possibly break a leg so that I would not have to face up to his death. I could pretend that he was still alive and just in another room from me. I felt like my chest was ripping apart with the pain. Even though I wanted the coward's way out, I knew that it wasn't possible. Paul's death had to be faced. Somehow we got through that night. Paul was a beautiful sight. Katherine had bought him a beautiful two pieced white suit for him to be buired in. It had short pants and the top of the pants buttoned onto the bottom of the shirt. He looked just like he was sleeping. When I stared at him hard enough, I could imagine that I could see him breathing, his little chest rising and falling. I kept thinking that he was not dead. It had just been a cruel trick. His short red hair shown like a halo and the dimples in his knees and hands looked just like they did when I played on the foor with him and kissed each one of them. He looked beautiful and he was my baby and I wanted him back. The choice was no longer mine.

I remember the day of the funeral just like it was yesterday. It was a bright sun shiny day. I thought how unfair of the sun to shine so brightly when my whole world had fallen apart. On the ride to the cemetery, following the hearse, I saw children running and playing in the street. Some of them were dirty and had on torn and tattered clothing. My thoughts were that why would God take a child that was loved so much when these children appeared to have no one who cared about them. George and I supported each other during these trying times. When I was down the most, he would be the strong one, and I became the strong one when he was down. We somehow muddled through.

Bernie Hambrice

   While our house was being rebuilt, we lived in Eastern New Orleans in a place called Maison Michou Apartments. Our lives became somewhat settled, but I was forever counting 1, 2, 3, 4 – never again 5. I kept a sharp eye on the children because I was so afraid. I know that I must have driven them pretty crazy. They were not allowed to be out of my sight. Jerry went through a harder time it seemed. He had been 2 when Paul was born and he considered it his job to take care of Paul. We thought that we had done the right thing telling him that he was the bigger brother. Mark had been the big brother to Fern so Jerry had been Paul's bigger brother. After the fire and Paul's death, Jerry would panic if I got out of his sight. One day we had to go and buy new furniture. The house was almost ready. Jerry went into a screaming fit when I told him that we had to go shopping and that he was going to stay with a friend. He held on to my skirt sobbing and sobbing. Finally he said, "Mom – promise me that you won't die and leave me like Paul did. Promise me that you will come back to get me if you die." I realize now that all of the children should have had counseling, but at that time, it wasn't what was on my mind.

   We managed to live each day one at a time – just like the song says. I was still feeling depressed and spent a lot of time crying when no one was around. I remember sitting in a bathtub full of water and thinking how easy it would be to sink down in the water and just let go. Then I would think of George and our other children. Many night I cried into my pillow to keep George from hearing me. Finally the pain was so bad that I couldn't breathe. I lay in bed fighting for breath and hurting like someone was ripping my chest into shreds with a dull knife. That night I did what I should have done in the first place. I prayed to God. I asked Him for help. I explained how I could no longer handle the pain by myself. I felt that if I didn't get to hold my child, Paul, one more time that I would surely just curl up and die. After I prayed, I fell into a very deep sleep. That night I dreamed that I was holding Paul in my arms. I hugged and kissed him and squeezed him like there was no tomorrow. While I was holding him, a young girl from our neighborhood came up and asked why Paul was so white. I explained to her that Paul had died and that God was letting me borrow him back one more time so that I could hold and kiss him. All night in my dreams I held Paul. He never said a word. I just couldn't seem to get enough touching and kissing him. When I awoke the next morning, God had truly answered my prayers. That tremendous feeling of hurt had disappeared and I was at peace. I thank God for being so gracious to me. He has never let me down.

Life went on. We found joy and peace again. We knew that God had taken a special interest in our family and that everything would be all right. We could never replace Paul, but God gave us other blessings. Some of them we weren't sure were blessings, but when we look back, we know that they were. The first of these was when I wanted to get a foster child. At first, George said no. He was afraid that we were leaving ourselves open for more heartbreak. He was never able to hold out against me very long. He finally agreed. We went through the necessary steps and were approved as foster parents. They told us that they could send us a little boy 9 years old. We were happy with that decision. First, they told us that the child, Leroy, had a slight speech impediment – it turned out to be severe. As the time for us to get Leroy came closer, they told us that he was a little slow in learning – it turned out that he was on a 2-3 year old mental level. Then the night before they were to bring Leroy to us, they told us that he had supposedly burned a house down in Texas. We looked at each other fearfully, but agreed to still take the child.

The next day Leroy was brought to us and that began a whole new chapter in our lives. George had to go to work that night. He did shift work at the refinery at that time. I always thought that I was a light sleeper because of an attempted break in a few years earlier. I thought that I slept with one ear continually listening for every sound. I could picture me lying on my side and the ear that was up rotating around like a radar device, picking up each and every sound. Somehow that night my radar let me down. I slept soundly and when I got up the next morning there was surprise after surprise waiting for me. I noticed that the gold colored carpet in the living room had big black blotches on it. I guess that my eyes were opened really wide at that point. I went into the kitchen and there was some kind of goop all over the floor in front of the refrigerator. I opened the door and there was a big bowl with a towel in it and the towel was dripping the same sticky substance. Puzzled as I was, it was still too early in the morning for coherent thought. I thought to go to the bathroom before solving all of these mysteries. When I lifted the lid to the commode, I saw about 17 cigarette butts in the bowl. Now I was really concerned! Where had all of this stuff come from and who had put it there? I guess my "What the" woke Leroy up. He was so happy to see me. He said that he had a surprise for me – that he had fixed breakfast. Well, that solved the kitchen mess. It turned out that he had mixed all of the milk, all of the eggs (shells and all), coffee grounds and Dream Whip together to make breakfast. It was spilling and that is why he put the towel on (in) the bowl. So much for mess #1. Then I asked him if he knew who had been smoking cigarettes. He smiled happily and said, "Me did, Mama." I was shocked and asked him where had he gotten the cigarettes. He told me that he had stood on a chair; undid the chain lock; and went across the street to a neighbor's car and took the cigarettes. Surprise #2 solved. With my amazing powers of deduction, I was suddenly able to solve the third surprise. The big black blotches on the carpet were burns where he had dropped matches and/or cigarettes (remember the house in Texas). When asked if he smoked (remember 9 year old child – 2-3 year old mental level) in his other foster home; he looked at me proudly and said, "Me other foster mother let me drink beer and smoke." I assured him that this mama was not going to let that happen again and if he wanted to keep his happy home with us; he had better not even think about it.

Things settled down a little after that. We soon learned to not send Holly out to find Leroy when we didn't know where he was. Her idea of finding Leroy was to stand in the middle of the yard and shout, "Foster boy, oh foster boy, where are you?" Leroy had a way of keeping things in a turmoil whether he wanted to or not. It got easy for neighbors to blame him for things that he couldn't have possibly done. Like the time one of the neighbors swore that he had taken her car keys out of the ignition earlier that day and lost them. One of her children said that they had seen him in the car. We had been gone from home all that day until just before she had come down to make the accusation. We quickly learned that Leroy was capable of plenty things on his own. He didn't need any help. I remember one of the worse things that happened shortly before we decided to put our house up for sale. Our next door neighbor, Carol, had an outside utility room that opened onto her carport. She had a habit of piling her dirty laundry in the utility room. Leroy was outside riding his bike and I thought that all was well. He came inside shortly and said that he had helped Miss Carol. I said that he couldn't have been helping her because she wasn't home. He said, "Me been helping her wash clothes." Shudders went through my body with every breath as I ran out of the front door and over to her house. Leroy had put all of the dirty clothes, white, dark, permanent press, jeans and towels into the washer. He poured all of the soap powder in the box into the washer and somehow managed to turn it on. I had to be careful not to slip in the bubbles cascading down the washer and the driveway. I managed to turn the water off just as she drove into her driveway. There, I was caught redhanded, but I suppose that she might have possibly figured it out on her own. We started looking for a house to buy several miles away after that. She was not unhappy to see us move.

We moved into our house on Gallo Drive and there the saga of Leroy continues. He was always doing the unexpected. He took George's coin collection and gave parts of it to his friends at school. He threw a Frisbee on the roof of the house next door. When it wouldn't come down, he threw a ballpeen hammer up to knock it down. It didn't make it as far as the roof. It went through their sliding glass window. When the same neighbor's oldest son graduated from school, they bought him a truck. That truck was Bobby's pride and joy. Well, he had the bad sense to park it in the driveway behind another car. Leroy wanted to ride his bike on the sidewalk, so he got into the truck and somehow managed to get it out of gear and it rolled out into the street. Thank goodness no cars were coming down the street. After that, we tried to be even more careful about where Leroy was and what he was doing, but Leroy learned to sneak out of a window. This time he got into another neighbor's pickup truck and did the same thing. This time it just rolled into a utility pole, but no damage was done except to our reputations. I thought that we were going to have to move again.

When we moved to Gallo Drive and enrolled our children in school, Mark and Fern went to Trist Middle School; Jerry and Leroy went to Lacoste Elementary and Holly went to Our Lady of Lourdes Pre-school. I had started at the St. Bernard Community College that year (the year that the school began) and wanted to pursue a degree in elementary education, During the second semester that the college was open, George started to school there also. We were all going different ways at different times. The only time that we were all together as a family was at breakfast and after school hours – but only if George was not on the evening shift.

The Fall after we began living on Gallo, Rose and Bruce came to visit. She asked me to go out and see what she had in her car. She was forever taking in stray cats and dogs. I told her that I really didn't feel like walking out to her car to see another animal, but she kept insisting. When we got to the car, there was a baby girl asleep on the front seat. She was 11 months old. Rose told me that she was baby sitting with her and that the baby's mother would come and get her on the weekends. She was a precious child, but I already 4 precious children of my own and Leroy to take care of.

Rose, Bruce and the baby girl, Samantha, came over on New Year's Eve. It was one of the coldest nights of the year. I asked Rose if she was sure that the baby would be warm enough in their house down in Hopedale because the house was not properly heated. She and I talked and planned to have the baby spend the night with us as they were coming back the next day for New Year's dinner. George got the baby bed out of the attic and we kept Samantha that night and the next. By then, we were hooked. Rose told us that she was no longer able to take care of the baby because Bruce needed her help. He was an oyster fisherman and needed her to go on the boat with him. I asked George if we could keep the baby and he said no. He was afraid that we would get too attached to her and when the mother decided that she wanted her back, we would be devastated. Finally, after much sulking and pouting, I was able to convince him. Rose got in touch with the birth mother, JoAnn Guidry, who had not come back to get the baby, and asked her if she would sign papers giving us custody of Samantha. She agreed and came to our house so that we could all go to the lawyer's office and sign the papers. We then had to go before a judge, have her declared abandoned and put in our care. After a few months, we went before a judge to get the adoption process started. A year after that we were able to go to court and finalize the adoption. We had one problem that tested our patience. Samantha had 2 birth certificates, one with father unknown, and a second one a month later stating the father was Tillman Pietre. When notified by our lawyer and asked to sign a release, he refused. Even though we had a new birth certificate for Samantha Marie Hambrice, listing her parents as George and Bernie

Life As I Know It

Hambrice, we were not able to get her a social security number. That was not a real problem at the time, but frustrated her when, as a teenager, she wanted to get a job. She had to wait until she was 18 to apply for her card.

All this time I was still going to school. Most of my classes were in the daytime when the children were in school – that is all but Samantha. I had George watch her when he was at home, but if he was working I had to find someone else. When I had evening classes and George was at work, my poor mom usually had the privilege of watching all 6 children. She did this after teaching school all day and trying to help Kathy and Buddy with their homework and also fix supper for the family. She wanted me to get a degree so badly that she would have agreed to almost anything.

I finally graduated from Our Lady of Holy Cross College in 1974, but I had gotten a job teaching at Meraux School before I completed my student teaching. So I was working before graduation. Thank goodness. Those were hard years. Not only did we have to buy school clothes and supplies for the children, but we had to do the same for me, plus paying tuition. George was so happy when I finally got to work and had a regular paycheck coming in. Samantha started to school that Fall and Geeorge was in heaven. Not only did we have the extra paycheck, but now he was free during the day when he wasn't at work. He began going to movies and out to eat with friends. He actually tried to hide these facts from me, but I told him like I told our children – that there wasn't much that went on with my family that I didn't know about. He felt like he had a new lease on life because during part of the time before I went to work; he worked 2 jobs. I really don't know how he did it. He would only get 3 or 4 hours of sleep most days. The Good Lord got us through those days.

As we got older, our lives got easier. George could now enjoy his job and take part in other activities and I loved my job of teaching. Sometimes I thought that I should be paying the school board because I got so much enjoyment from teaching. Every day was a new experience – not only with school, but also with my family. It was strange to realize that our babies were growing up so quickly. The years slipped by and before we knew it they were in their teens. We watched with pride as each one of them developed into the wonderful adults they became.

Bernie Hambrice

We were so proud of each one for a different reason. My children have been my pride and one of the greatest blessings that God has given me.

One of the things that tilted our world was that George developed diabetes while in his late thirties. He thought that because he was so big (6'3" and about 285 pounds) the disease wouldn't hurt him. He did not take his insulin injections like he was suppose to and this caused further problems. He had a heart attack and was in the hospital for a good while. The damage to his heart caused him to have a quadruple by-pass. Other problems followed and in 1989, he was declared legally blind and had to take long term disability and then disability retirement. His health continued on a downward slide and in February, 1992, he had to go on kidney dialysis. That July, he became confined to a wheelchair. The quality of his life was bad. He was legally blind, needed a new heart valve, unable to work, and on dialysis. The life he now led was such that he began to pray to die. On September 25, 1992, his prayers were answered. We wept, but we had to say, "Thank You, Lord". His pain and misery had been so intense, that we had to be thankful that it had ended.

I continued to teach school until the end of May 2000. I officially retired in August of that year, after teaching at Meraux Elementary for 25 years and 1 year at Joe Davies Elementary. Traveling has now become my career and working has become my hobby. I really don't have a lot of time for my hobby though. God has given me a great life with 5 wonderful children; sons-in-law Steve and Dwayne; daughters-in-law Mary and Jean; and grandchildren, Jennifer, Paul, Jeff, Jill, Theresa, Suelynn, Sydney, and Cassidy. I continue to live on Gallo Drive in Chalmette, but have plans to move to Mountain Home, Arkansas in the near future if the Good Lord is willing. This story of my life was completed in January, 2001.

MAY GOD GIVE YOU AS MANY BLESSINGS AS HE HAS GIVE ME

AND NOW FOR THE REST OF THE STORY

Life As I Know It

Bernie Hambrice

THE REST OF THE STORY

Oh, where to begin? I really have to backtrack down memory lane. It has been 19 years since my son asked for my story and I wrote the first part. Now, I am trying to figure out where to begin. All of our children have grown up and have given me more wonderful grandchildren. We have added Jordan, Jared, Katie, and Kelsey to the grandchildren count.

When I decided to move to Arkansas, I sold my house on Gallo Drive to Jerry and Jean. Then I was off and running. I found my dream home up in the mountains in a place called Cherokee Village, Arkansas. It was only about 5 or 6 miles from the home of Mark, Mary, and Theresa. Jerry and my brother, Buddy packed up a moving truck and my pickup and like the Beverly Hillbillies we set out.

We arrived at the new house on September 10. It was late so we only unpacked the mattresses so we would have a place to sleep that night. We made it through the night and Mark came over that morning to give us a helping hand. We were unloading when I got a call on my cell phone from Holly. She said that an airplane had just hit the twin towers in New York. I didn't realize the severity of what was happening. A short time later, she called to tell me that a second plane had hit the other tower. We didn't have the TV connected, so we still had no idea what was happening. Mary was fixing lunch for us over at their house and when we finally got to see television, the reality of what had happened suddenly hit home. We sat watching the drama unfold until we had to go back to my house to finish unpacking so that Jerry and Buddy could head back home to Chalmette. The 9/11 horror became very real and I would sit and watch rescue efforts with tears streaming down my face. I have no words to describe the horror, anguish, and pain that we, Americans, were feeling. All we could say was, "God bless America."

Life As I Know It

My house was my fortress. It had 6 sets of French doors so I was able to see outside no matter where I was in the house. I was impatient for my first lightening/thunder storm so I could watch God's fury and still be safe inside. Then I could hardly wait for my first snowfall. I heaped logs in the giant fireplace to be ready to enjoy the beauty of outdoors while snug in my warm and comfortable house. The first snow finally came and I realized that I had become a prisoner in my own home. The house was located in the foothills of the Ozark Mountains and my driveway with snow and ice had become a giant slide. The beauty was worth the problem for the first snow event, but when it was forecast the next time, I went to visit my friend, Kathleen Cooper, at Scott Valley Ranch in Mountain Home.

Many miles were driven during the time that I lived in that house. I made trips back and forth to Chalmette every time one of the grandchildren had an event. Bro. John announced in church that I was just like weeds, always showing up. I didn't want to miss any events in their lives. They were much too important to me for that. After all, they were God's blessings. Also two baby showers were given that I had to attend. This is when Jordan and Jared made their appearances in the world.

On one of the trips back to Chalmette, I realized that I really needed to move home and be more of a part of our growing family. Mark took care of renting my house in Cherokee Village and then selling it for me. I sold my house there in 2005, and was living in the house that had been my Aunt Katherine's and Uncle Ralph's home. Holly now owned it and I was making needed repairs. Paul lived in one of the bedrooms and later on Buddy moved in too.

This takes us to August 2005. Television and radio report kept telling us about an impending storm that was headed to Florida or Alabama. I was with a lot of my church friends at a retreat in Lumberton, Mssissippi when we were told that the storm had turned away from Florida and appeared to be heading for the Louisiana coast. We headed back to Chalmette from the retreat only to pack up and leave for higher ground. Holly and Robin had made reservations in northern Mississippi on the Tennessee border. This storm, Hurricane Katrina, devestated St. Bernard Parish, which was 97% under water. We watched the television in horror as only the rooftops of our area were visible above the water. Even people in 2 story houses had to exit by cutting holes in their roofs. I kept remembering the passage from "The Ancient Mariner" - "Water, water everywhere and all the boards did shrink. Water, water everywhere and not a drop to drink." This was at the end of August. Because of allergies, I was not able to return to St. Bernard Parish Until February 2006. We were living with Fern and Steve in their house in Carriere. Mississippi, and drove down to survey the damage. People from all over America and Canada had come as volunteers to muck out houses and help in any way that they could. The world had come together again just as it had after the 9/11 attack.

The hardest part of seeing St. Bernard again was to see all of my possessions, both household and personal piled up in a trash heap in front of the house. Life as we knew it, had again changed. I only had renter's insurance, so nothing was covered by insurance. Praise God, He always takes care of our needs and the wants are up to us. I found that there was hardly anything lacking in my life that I wanted. I was able to secure a SBA loan, buy a mobile home and put it in Holly's yard in Carriere. The whole episode has been glossed over and I can finally count it as another learning experience. Thanks be to God for making us resilant.

While I was livng there, Samantha, Sydney, and Cassidy moved in with Holly, Robin, Debbie, and the kids. They wanted to go to high school away from Chicago. Dwayne later moved in and got a good job doing what he loved, cook and dye making. They lived in Mississippi for the girl's first year of high school, but found a house to rent in Louisiana in a good school district. They remained in Abita Springs until the girls graduated from high school and looking forward to entering college. Sydney was going to LSU and Cassidy was going to Southeastern so Sam and Dwayne found another rental close to where they both worked.

Sydney wanted to go into the nursing program. She lived in Baton Rouge during the week, but returned home on the weekends and worked at the Audubon Zoo in New Orleans. Cassidy lived in the dorm in Hammond during the week, but also went home for the weekends. Sydney had been dating a man named Jatory Evans and was expecting his child. In the beginning he was very protective of Sydney, but as time went on, he became very possessive and dictatorial with her. He tried to alienate her from her family and friends. So finally, at 7 months pregnant, she had to have him served with a restraining order. By this time, he had cut the tires on her car and poured bleach into her gas tank. He was harassing her day and night. Finally she has all she could stand.

Sydney was well loved by her co-workers at the zoo and they planned a baby shower for her on November 7th. Cassidy was planning to cut classes that day to share this event with Sydney, but she found that she had a test scheduled. She called Sydney to tell her that she needed to stay at school for the test and asked if that would be ok. It was on the same day that Jatory and his cousin in Baton Rouge rented a car for the day. Jatory used the car to drive to Metairie where the Hanson family lived. He somehow got into the house and repeatedly attacked Sydney with a knife. Samantha and Dwayne left work to go get lunch and went home to eat it. When Dwayne went into the house on this stormy day, he was shot in the back of his head and killed. Jatory went after Samantha. He chased her out into the pouring rain; shot her 5 times, and stabbed her 20 plus times. She died, lying face down in the pouring rain on the ground. This monster went back inside the house and upstairs to Sydney's room. He put papers over her and set her on fire. This is what I have been told. Thankfully he was arrested the next day by the Jefferson Parish Police Department and brought to jail where he was questioned. The deputies told us how arrogant he was.

The family went from stunned belief to finally accepting the painful loss we had just suffered. We planned and held a memorial service for the family that had brutally been taken from us. The outpouring of sympathy and concern was overwhelming. Once again our hearts were shattered, but God held us together and covered us with His love. God was in control and was watching over us. We were so thankful that Cassidy's life had been spared. So many prayers of thanksgiving have been lifted for her. Justice was complete about 9 months later. I was traveling with friends when I received a wonderful phone call that Jatory had taken his own life while in jail. I felt like the weight of the world had been lifted off of my shoulders. His family never reached out to us after the murders and has now filed a law suit against the Jefferson Parish Police Department because he was not still on suicide watch. Haven't cared enough to find out if or how much money they were given in this farce.

Bernie Hambrice

    As the song says, "life goes on" and we eagerly faced each day. Then almost 2 years later, another shock wave threw me to the ground. I was planning a trip to spend time in Arkansas with Mark, Mary, and their friend, Judy, from Scotland. It was going to be Judy's birthday and we had plans to help her celebrate. Mark had recently had a weight reduction surgery and I was anxous to see the difference in him. As I returned from a doctor's visit, Jerry greeted me at the door. He had sent the children next door to get them out of the house. He told me to have a seat and that we needed to talk. I had no idea what he was going to say. Jerry simply said, "Mark didn't make it." I stupidly said, "Didn't make what" and then the expressn on his face told me all that I needed to know. I had just lost another child. God, in His infinite mercy, gave me the strength to hold together once again.

    It is now January when I am writing the rest of the story and I am 82 years old. My prayer is simply that before another of my children leave this Earth, my death will come before their's. I am ready to meet my Savior face to face and to be reunited with all that have gone before. May God's blessings fill your life and help to turn all of your tests into testimonies.

    P.S. Please take the time to read some of my writings at the end of this and look at the faces in the pictures shared. God bless!

Life As I Know It

Bernie Hambrice

IS GOD REAL?

At least once in every person's life, they will ask the question " IS GOD REAL?" Once in a Sunday School class, the teacher asked me the question, "How do you know that God is real?" Witout hesitation, I answered that it says so in the Bible. She then stated that the Bible is only a book and that anyone could write a book and put anything they wanted in it, but would that make it true.

I thought for a minute or two pondering the question and wondering what I could say that would prove that God is indeed real. I began to recall the experience in my life that could answer her original question.

I was very fortunate that God had chosen to give me five beautiful, healthy children. They were everything to me and my life centered around them and my husband. One fateful night, God chose to take one of them back to live with Him on high. He was the one that demanded the most of my attention – a red headed two year old who was a bundle of love.

The hurt that haunted me day and night was unreal. Sometimes it seemed to be more than I could bear. My arms hurt with the need to hold his sweet little body close to mine; to hear his thrilling laughter as we argued over the ownership of his seven month old sister. I began to think how easy it would be to take own life – to slip down under the water when taking a bath and then once again be reunited with my child. One night I was in the bathtub and had cried so long and hard that my body became limp with fatigue. I actually slipped down under the water and held my breath until I began to lose consciousness. Suddenly the image of my other beautiful children and husband came in to my mind and I began to struggle to get up from under the water. After what seemed to be an eternity, I was able to sit up, gasping for air.

Life As I Know It

I knew then that I could no longer handle my grief alone. That night I prayed to God. I asked Him to help me handle the unbearable pain that I was feeling; to help lessen the crushing hurt that haunted me every minute of every day.

I fell asleep that night with teardrops soaking my pillow as I buried my face in the pillow to stifle the sobs. All during my sleep that night, I held my precious little boy once again. During the dream, I saw a neighboring child come up to us. She played with my little boy, Paul, while I held him. She asked, "Why is Paul so white?" I replied, "Gayle, you know that Paul died, but God let me borrow him back because I miss him so much. The dream seemed to go on forever as I held his little body close to me and smothered him with love and kisses. My arms were filled with his lively little body and my heart was filled with love. The next morning, I awoke to a feeling of peace and contentment. My arms no longer ached and my heart no longer seemed to be ripping in shreds.

As I related this to the Sunday School class, a warm loving feeling of total contentment washed over me. Then I had the answer to her question. I know that God is real because He is part of me and my life; just as much as my head, my arms, legs and other body parts. Without Him I would be incomplete, still hurting, and looking for solace. Now I can say to the world, "God is love and GOD IS INDEED REAL!"

Bernie Hambrice

WALKING ON WATER

    Bible stories have always been a part of my life and there are many that stand out. Do you remember the one, "Jesus walks on Water"? Jesus had his disciples get in a boat to cross the water while He stayed behind and prayed. A storm came up with the wind blowing ferociously and the waves tossed the boat about. The men in the boat saw a figure walking on the water and coming toward them. They thought it was a ghost. Jesus called out to them, "It s I. Do not be afraid." They were skeptical and Peter said, "If you are really Jesus, let me walk out to you." Jesus said, "Come" and Peter started walking out to Him. But when he looked down at the tossing waves, he became afraid and began to sink.

    My story begins on another stormy night, November 7, 2016. I was living in Mississippi, but was visiting with my friend, Zay, in Chalmette who was telling me that the weather was too bad to make the 60 mile trip to Mississippi that night and was inviting me to spend the night at her house. We were laughing and talking when my cell phone rang. It was a relative asking me if I had spoken to my daughter, Samantha, that day. I told her that because she was at work, I hadn't spoken to her. She advised me to stay where I was and hung up. A little later, another relative called me and told me that there was a fire in Samantha's area and that 2 people were dead.

    I immediately tried to find the number for the Jefferson Parish's Sheriff's Office, but couldn't locate it. I called the Sheriff's Office in Chalmette and asked if they could find the number for me. They said that they would connect me with them. When they came on the line, I asked about the fire, but in my confusion. I reversed the numbers for their house address and they said it was not at that address. Just then, my daughter-in-law, Jean, came in and said that it was their house. We quickly turned the television on and it was on the news. They said that two bodies had been found – one in the house and one in the yard. My whole world came tumbling down and I fell apart.

Even as I sit here writing this, the pain of that moment returns. I can hardly see the computer screen with the hot tears streaming down my face. My heart breaks all apart with the memories of what was yet still to come.

My daughter, Holly, had just gotten back to the airport from a birthday celebration in Key West when she found out and came straight to Chalmette to get me. As we drove home that night, the rain was pouring down like God was shedding tears for the tragedy. Mine and His mingled together on the long ride as I tried to make sense of what was going on. They said that the two people, Samantha and Dwayne, had been shot. They did not die because of the fire. I wondered where their twenty year old twin daughters were. I finally heard that Cassidy, one of the twins, had been at the Jefferson Parish Sheriff's Office and then had gone to Jenny's (another granddaughter) house.

We finally found out that after the fire had been put out, they found another body in the house. That was Sydney, the other twin, who was 7 months pregnant. All night I cried and rocked back and forth like I could shake it all away. The reality and horror washed over me with every breath like the stormy waves attacking the shore in a hurricane. I relived every moment that they must have endured. My daughter had been shot 5 times and stabbed over 20 times and she was found in the yard lying in the pouring rain. Dwayne had been shot in the back of the head and was in the kitchen. Sydney was upstairs in her bedroom and had been stabbed repeatedly. She had been covered with paper and set on fire while she was still breathing.

We eventually learned that the crime had been committed by Sydney's ex-boyfriend whom she had just gotten a restraining order for. He was arrested the next day and finally justice was done nine months later when he committed sucide in his jail cell.

This is when I began to walk on water. You see, I had learned a vavuable lesson from Peter when he tried to walk on water. He failed because he took his eyes off of Jesus and looked down. I will live in His love and always keep me eyes on Him. Through God, all things are possible.

THE LIGHTHOUSE THAT AWAYS SHINES

Have you ever felt defeated and lost like the light has gone out of your life? I want to share with you the story of my source of light – a Lighthouse that never grows dim or goes out. This is about my own personal Lighthouse that we are talking about.

Many of us knows the joy of motherhood and what a special blessing it is. Each birth is a miracle created by God and holds a special place in the depth of our hearts. I was fortunate to have five lovely bundles of joy given to me and one that was given to be through adoption. I felt so very blessed. You may know that God took one back when he was just two years old. The pain at that time was unbearable or so I thought. Then 3 years ago, a monster of a human being took my adopted daughter, her husband, one of their daughters, and a soon to be born great granddaughter lives. Again the shredding of my heart took place.

Last year, I was joyfully planning a trip to Arkansas to spend time with my first born, his wife, and a friend from Scotland. My son had just had weight loss surgery two weeks before. He was so excited to show off the new "me" he had become. I had been to the cardiologist for my annual checkup and was feeling great that all was well. When I walked into the house after the appointment, my other son, Jerry, told me to sit down because he had something to say. He said, "Mark didn't make it." Stupidly I said, "Didn't make what?" Then the bottom of my world came to another sinking halt as I looked at his expression and could see the pain on his face. With an agonizing scream that came from the very pit of my soul, I finally understood what he meant. I collapsed and just kept reteating, "Why wasn't it me instead?" Again there was no answer. The pain, hurt, and sorrow seep through my veins into all of my being.

Life As I Know It

Once again, God took me in His loving arms and held me tight. That same God is my Lighthouse. He is always there to strengthen and comfort me. People always tell me that they don't know how I stood all the hurt and sorrow. But if you have a Lighthouse That Always Shines, the Light will continue to guide you through all storms and your ship will continue to sail.

Bernie Hambrice

FIRST ATTEMPT AT WRITING POETRY IN EIGHTH GRADE

School

School is good
And not very bad.
But going to school
Is what is sad.

I love my books,
I love my teachers,
But I would rather sit
Through a good double feature.

I love my books,
They are all so dear;
But for vacation time,
Let's all give a cheer!

POEM FROM TEACHING YEARS.

Expectations

He stood there looking as sad as anyone could be.
I wondered what it was he wanted from me.
He began to speak in a mournful tone
And tell me how he is so alone.
"My dad, he's been gone for over a year."
As he said this I saw the beginning of one little tear.
"My mom, she drinks and stays out most of the night.
And when she comes home we just seem to fight."
"I feel I have no one to call my very own,
I wonder if it's worth the effort to ever be grown."
His thin little body began to tremble and shake,
And before I knew it, my hand he began to take.
I, as his teacher, had his life in my hand.
That life could be better, he had to understand.
What could I do to have him trust in me –
That together we could make his future what it ought to be.
When all at once, we both had tears in our eyes,
He knew that between us there would be no lies.
I took him in my arms in the space of a minute,

Bernie Hambrice

And in the circle of my love he could feel safe in it.
It's an awesome responsibility that God has given me.
I pray that this love will somehow set him free.
Poem written in retirement years.

Night Sounds

The midnight hour had come and gone
And people slept and dreamed everywhere
When suddenly the mournful howl of a lone
Train horn split and tormented the silent air.
The clacking of the speeding wheels
Added to the other sounds
As the train raced through the night
To complete its scheduled rounds.
Lightening flashed and danced
Across the inky black sky;
Rumbling thunder crashed like crazed cymbals
And frightened dogs began to howl and cry.
And ever so softly a light rain
Whispered as it began to fall
Pittering-pattering upon the dry warm ground,
To let us know that greater storms would come to call.
The little green tree frogs began to sing
Their own lively special rain song
Beseeching the heaven for much more rain.
And they didn't have to wait too long.
The skies opened up with a great gush
And much harder rain began to fall,

Life As I Know It

As the large hard drops tap danced on the roof
And the wind blew the rain forceibly against the wall.
Just as the tempo reached its greatest heights,
Suddenly, it was over and quiet reigned over the land;
We had just experienced a soulful symphony
Orchestrated by God's own loving hand.

Photos Of My Past

Photos Of My Past

Bernie Hambrice

My Childhood Best Friend Ta Tee and Me

Life As I Know It

My Brother Patrick and Me

Patrick Lee McDaniel

Bernie Hambrice

Magnolia AR - 8 Months

15 Months

Homer LA – 2 Years   My Grandmother and Me – 3 Years

Bernie Hambrice

Springhill LA – 3rd Birthday

Life As I Know It

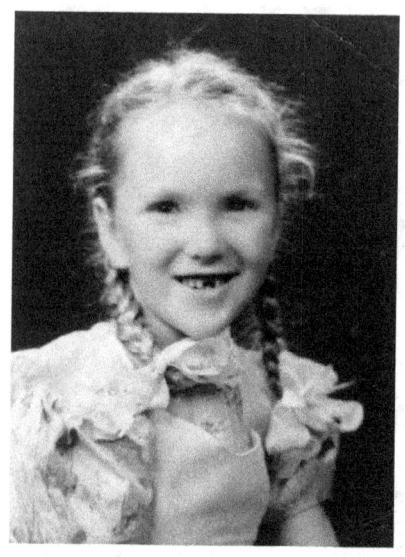

1st Grade   Junior Year

Wedding Day March 16, 1957

Bernie Hambrice

Front Row – Jerry, Fern, Mark
Back Row – Myself, Paul, George

Bernie Hambrice

ST. BERNARD PARISH CHAPTER
CHARTERED 1918

American Red Cross

Bernie Hambrice
Volunteer of the Year

ANNUAL MEETING AND AWARDS BANQUET
WEDNESDAY, NOVEMBER 9, 1988

Bernie Hambrice

THE FAMILY TREE

GEORGE'S PARENTS
Hurbert H Hambrice   Paunee P Cloud Hambrice

BERNIE'S PARENTS
Meak B McDaniel Sr   Fern Carroll McDaniel

US
George G Hambrice   Bernie C McDaniel Hambrice

CHILDREN AND SPOUSES
Mark E Hambrice   Mary L Crissman Hambrice
Fern C Hambrice Acosta   Steven E Acosta
Jerry L Hambrice   Jean A Corley Hambrice
Paul D Hambrice (deceased)
Holly K Hambrice Bryson   Robin L Bryson
Samantha M Hambrice Hanson   Dwayne A Hanson

FOSTER CHILD
Leroy Poole

GRANDCHILDREN
Jennifer L Acosta Reeb   Ryan Reeb
Paul D Hambrice
Jeffrey S Acosta   Jessica G Acosta
Jill Acosta Reynolds   Cody Reynolds
Suelynn A Corley
Theresa M Hambrice Hill   Nathan Hill
Sydney T Hanson
Cassidy N Hanson
Jordan O Bryson
Jared Bryson
Katie L Hambrice
Kelsey J Hambrice

GREAT GRANDCHILDREN
Gavin Reeb, Stella Reeb, Asher Acosta, Caden Acosta, Josie Acosta
Lyla Reynolds, Logan Reynolds, Lucy Reynolds, Joey Heuber

MERCI BEAUCOUP

Life As I Know It

Many, many thanks to my pastor, John Dee Jeffries who made this possible.

To Carol Stockton Saling who helped by keeping me within the guidelines and scanning pictures.

To my wonderful family for always being there when I needed them most.

And to my Lord and Savior, Jesus Christ, who walked with me every step of my life.

Bernie Hambrice

Life As I Know It

Bernie Hambrice